WHEN A JAILBIRD SINGS

"The Birth Of A Poet"

Daniel La'Mot Smith

TABLE OF CONTENTS

Acknowledgements

First, I want to honor my Lord and Savior, who has enabled me, through strength and wisdom, to expound on one of my favorite gifts. My experiences from a child, to a young man and now as an adult has allowed me to navigate through different physical and mental aspects about life and love. Indulge with me as you read these experiences and allow your heart to be open, feel the pain as you imagine yourself in the same state of expressed emotions. From "An Image of Reality", as I compared my love for writing to a woman's touch, to "The Dream that Didn't Come True", the only poem that appeared to me in the sky as if it was written just for me and as I end the book with a little sexually healing "Food for the Soul".

Second, I would like to thank my lovely and beautiful wife Nicole, for her endless words of wisdom and unwavering support. To my loving family and close friends, your support and prayers has allowed me to be strong and to keep the faith when I felt like giving up.

Lastly, it does take a village to raise a child, and this child grew up to become honored and grateful for his village. Words are only a mere gesture of how I really feel, and I hope that throughout my life and this book, I have returned what has been given to me so freely.

An Image of Reality

My nights were filled with hopes and dreams of seeing you,

But images were all that I saw, so I tried to figure out what I was going to do.

So, sitting at my desk, I closed my eyes and began to write,

I wrote about what we shared and how it felt so good throughout my entire night.

I thought about every hour, minute, and second of you being here,

Praying to God that this image of beauty would never ever disappear.

I thought about your touch, with means of healing a lost soul,

I thought about your eyes, as fire burned in them, ready to explode,

As with every breath you took, I took two trying not to lose,

Becoming what I knew as intimacy, hoping I didn't act like a fool.

But the night went so soft and smoothly, like her touch against my flesh,

Could this be what I wanted or was my maturity being put to the test?

Nevertheless, I still think that this is one test I did pass,

Hoping that the reality of this night will be the first and not the last.

A New Love for Me

Writing is like music to me; I love it in every which way,

I think about this special tune throughout my stressful day.

Just wanting to pick up a pencil and begin to draw this form of art,

Confused at first, but thoughts come as I begin to start.

The sound the lead makes when it hits the paper is like music to my ears,

Hearing the pad speak to me in words only I understand, asking me to stay near.

It excites me to write about love in every form, shape, and size,

My feelings are revealed because writing brings them alive.

When I sit to make love to these pages day after day,

I never get tired, because they love me back in a very special way.

Then reading what I wrote is a blessing to me,

A gift so hidden, but bright, it's like I'm the only one who can see.

Doing this thing called writing, is an art of expressed emotions,

As my heart and mind are welded through an experience of biological convolution.

A Mother to All (Iris Smith)

A mother is someone you know who goes out of her way to care,

A mother is someone you know will always be there.

A mother is someone you know that can help you confront those fears,

A mother is someone you know that can combat with you, those sadden tears.

A mother is someone you know that is not like a sister or a brother,

A mother is someone you know that's unique, simply because she is a mother.

A mother is someone you know who can love and who can cry,

A mother is someone you know who can't stand to say the word goodbye.

A mother is someone you know that you can call your best friend,

A mother is someone you know you can trust from the beginning to the end.

Undetected Poet

Genetically known by my shape and the structure of my soul,

I only have a future to fulfill and a physical form that will soon unfold.

Being that I am a human and my actions are those from a hereditary trait,

Leaves me in the position of being part of this society, whether I give or take.

I've seen in the past years, smiles on the faces of people who hated me inside,

I've also seen tears in the eyes of disbelievers, even though their hurt is impossible to hide.

Traveling over these roads of opportunities, has led me to the road I travel on now,

Given to me was a guiding light, along with strength and a peaceful smile.

I've felt love through kisses and hugs, but none of them claimed to be a friend to me,

The beginning of my life was happier, when I was most loved, I miss the love of family.

They would hold my pain, no matter how troubled or worried I may seem,

They offered to give me their life, but I just couldn't read the lines and what fell in between.

I took my life to the extreme, and ventured down a path I know nothing about,

Experiencing the pain and destruction, soon left me alone without a clue or doubt.

I struggled every day, to find what was the right thing for me to do,

Being that I saw no future in my life, I instantly began to feel sad and blue.

Thinking that everything and everyone was the blame for my everyday problems,

I couldn't seem to find any answers, so I started to isolate myself from all of them.

I started with my friends and then with the family that I loved so much,

Lastly it was myself, not recognizing the feeling from my own personal touch.

My head would hang low, like a child's lip when his favorite toy is taken away,

My disturbed life was my unclaimed future, now listen to what I'm about to say.

A night came to where I laid peacefully like a baby in its mother's arms,

My thoughts were undetected which caused my actions to do the worst of harm.

Being that my eyelids stayed closed, I'm sure I've seen this figure bright as day,

It placed something on my chest and said, "This is here to stay".

Without fear, I focused my eyes downwards to see what I had received,

Something that was already a part of me, was given to me again and I just couldn't believe.

My thoughts turned into questions, as my eyes began to see this muscular organ,

What is happening to me, I thought, am I who they really say I am.

I sat up abruptly, wiping the sweat off the top of my head,

For a minute, I believed my life was over and my dream to be a poet was all of a sudden misled.

I reached helplessly, for the ornament that was placed heavily upon my chest,

Nothing was found so I began to lie down again and rest.

My first thought as I tried to rest, was to find my sword and shield,

The next thought was to write until I felt my lonely heart amended and healed.

So, I began to write about things of nature and the reconstruction of humans,

I just wrote whatever came to mind, placing the words in the best way that I can.

As I lost tract of time, realizing that I've been venting for over an hour,

I then began to look back over my life and how the problems came in and devoured.

Reminding myself of what my mother used to say about how God will deliver you only if you ask,

So, I got on my knees, bowed my head and began this endless task,

I asked for wisdom, I asked for guidance and for the pursuit of finding happiness,

Finishing up, with that in mind, I opened my eyes knowing that I will be truly blessed!

So, I smiled with pleasure thanking HIM for allowing me a chance to restart,

Now I remember what was given to me that night, He took and mended my broken heart.

Falling Into Words

As I fell beneath the cracks of Almost and Uncertain,

Persuasion told me to watch out when I met Beware,

He told me that Danger and Exit wanted to meet me.

I did not know what to do so I turned to Conscience and Advice, they said Belief and Faith were

the key ones to talk to and make sure to speak to Hope without Doubt..

Suddenly Instinct came into the picture and so did Sense. Not knowing that Self had two friends,

Strength and Hope.

Then before I knew it, Existence came in with Endurance followed by Trouble and Worry.

Now I had no choice but to turn to Love and ask, "Where is Beauty"?

To my surprise, up popped Happiness with Reassurance on his arm and as Optimist spoke,

Opinion had to put in his two cents, which caused Pessimist to pop out, releasing Deception and Deceit.

Sinister was called in by Vile, Wicked and their leader, Corruption.

Morals told me to stand with Strength and Faith, because they will always have your back.

Decision came in with Strategy causing, what would have been a beat down, a fair and even fight.

Head-to-head we began, knocking down each other's opponents.

Morals, who was the leader, chose to use Strategy as an effective method.

At times, we felt that Discouragement would wear down our key factor, Awareness, but Faith and Strength stayed strong, causing Happiness to feel good that Reassurance was by our side.

As Understanding spoke about Misleading, Logic added that Reality played a major role in this battle,

And because of that, we had this Falling into Words.

My True Dream (Grandma Smith)

Remembering her is hard.

Instead, I chose to miss her.

Time is passing and so are my memories.

At the same time, I will never forget her.

Sometimes I wish for her back, but,

My selfishness will not allow me to act.

In this world of hatred and deceit.

Thank you God for taking her.

Help me, so that one day again we will meet!

My Authenticity

I want to write with all of me,

I want to write whether I am confined or free.

I want to write in the morning before the sun peaks,

I want to write all day, until I fall asleep.

I want to write about society and how it works,

I want to write about flowers, animals and the earth.

I want to write about love and everything within,

I want to write about war and how it feels to win.

I want to write about my family and how I love them all,

I want to write about the females, who expect me to always call.

I want to write about my job and how unrepentant my coworkers can be,

I want to write about those in the pursuit of being loved and just want to feel happy.

I want to write about those who are less fortunate than I,

I want to write about those who are being abused and how the fear is embodied in their eyes.

I want to write about those whose freedom is no longer a chance,

I want to write about love and the importance of giving romance.

I want to write about those who have the same love for this art,

I want to write about those who've paved the way so that I can create my mark.

I just want to write from my mind, body and my soul,

I just want to write so those who read can relate and inside they gravitate and take hold.

I just want to write simple messages so those who read can understand,

I want to write, I want to write, I want to write, because this is who I am!

10 Months and We Never Became Friends

I remember the circumference of the bars, an inch thick, silver toned steel, stuck together in orderly form like pieces to a puzzle.

Matching floors came with it like the awaking of a rainy day just waiting for an accident to happen.

I've seen smiles quickly turned into frowns and the joys of hope and a promising future are instantly crushed, once behind these bars.

I would often feel discouraged, by the closing of these bars, while praying to the Lord asking him to give me strength, so that I may keep my head up.

I witnessed repetitive hurt in the eyes of those that looked similar to me, constantly looking to the stars and moon desperately in search of answers.

Grabbing those bars, I would wish my ten fingers were as strong as the compound that held them together. I suddenly felt the pain, the pain from those who stood in the same position I stood, ten dark skinned covered bones locked around two bars, face pressed, eyes focused downward with nothing in sight like a bottomless pit.

Searching for answers, answers they have no questions to, questions they thought they could answer, answers to questions no one asked.

A look so lost, a soul so battered, and in that moment no healing words could produce smiles and laughter.

So amongst these long, drawn-out, crushed futures, I instantly became another part of someone else's past and if these bars never responded to them,

Why did I think they would ever respond to me?

C.I.W.Y.W (Call it What You Want)

The animals are in love
and so are the plants,
The passing motorist are coupled
and togetherness holds a lamp.
Shoes are paired
and each ceiling has a floor,
The sun has the moon
and hinges hold a door.
The morning has the night
and body parts are paired in two,
So why is it that I have only me
instead of me having you?

I Pray Lord, I Pray

Away I have been
Miles and miles away,
From city to city
I pray Lord, I pray!
I've seen the changing of religions
Thoughts on my mind I dare not say,
Some I respect truthfully
I pray Lord, I pray!
Seeing the moon from a different angle
Watching tree limbs from a distance sway,
A different place true indeed
I pray Lord, I pray!
Cries I've heard through stares
Like pain that's there to stay,
I've begun my journey back home
I pray Lord, I pray!
Memories flash like the passing motorist
This had to be the day,
My mission is over and now I can rest
I prayed Lord, I prayed!

A Confident Race

I am gone
Watch me run,
See my flapping feet behind me
Reflecting off my neck is the sun.
A destination I knowest not
But somewhere I will be,
Just the thoughts I have
And my ability to be free.
As I run with the birds
The rain and wind become my friends,
My hair blows not
But soon my journey will come to an end.
Though my confidence and energy stands abreast
Determination is on my side,
For I am on my way
No more will I have to hide.
As obstacles arise
They try to place me last in this race,
To Him I will give all the praise
No matter what my finishing place.

My legs are beginning to feel weary
And my heart is racing in an uproar,
Being that I am the only one racing
The victory is given to me once more.

Remembering Is The Aftermath (Grandma Smith)

I woke up today with the thought
Of you never going away,
Your smile appeared like the morning sun
Lord, please help me to get through this tragic day.
You would talk and read to us
And teach us to play on those wooden keys,
I always felt a special love for only you
I beg of you, Lord please!
She would carry us to those fruitful sticky bushes
As we played in her shadow under the midday sun,
One by one she would instruct us how to pick
Not allowing us to leave until her job was done.
Her beauty I remembered so vividly
With that smile, suitable for a king,
In her, I would see many wonderful gifts
And I just knew she was the master of everything!
She never spared the rod
Or took favor to some,

If wrong was done in her eyes
Then that rod and you, became one.
As I look towards the heavens
And see a cloud that looks like her,
My vision is blurred by the blistering sun
I am unprepared for what is about to occur.
Memories of her will be viewed differently
But one thing, they will never go away
My memories of her is all I have
And I will never push them away.

An Imaginary Illusion

An imaginary illusion appeared to me one night just as I began to write,

I instantly jumped from my chair and thought, something is not right.

Trying to convince my conscience that this is reality, I slowly began to speak,

My words began to be arthritic, like human bones that are incapable or too weak.

Nothing rolled off my tongue as I raised my hand outward as an indication,

Trying to find a way to signal or some other form of communication.

My extended arm suddenly drew back when I'd noticed this image began to reply,

Mimicking my actions, a similar arm was raised and being brave was something I wasn't going to try.

So motionlessly we stood, toe-to-toe, stare to stare as I tried not to blink,

Watching my every move, this illusion without notice, stepped back and gave me a wink.

I smiled, pleased to know that our communications would have to be up to me,

So, I focused my eyes, took a step closer, now let me tell you of this imagery.

First I noticed, by being a man, that the gender was a different form than I,

I then began to look up in search of a hole in my ceiling to see if she fell from the sky.

Her hair then swayed peacefully like groups of clouds in mid-air,

As it reminded me of darkness and the thickness of fog, I felt myself starting to stare.

If I could ever describe the mixture of cocoa and a light shade of walnut, this would be the color of her eyes,

They had a welcoming glow to them and when she blinked you experienced a different surprise.

Her bosoms were rounded perfectly like ninety-nine cents to a dollar,

Making the rest of her body a complete structure, if you saw her you would just holla.

Her stomach matched her waist, which instantly brought a smile to my lips,

Then I couldn't believe what hung out back in between her hips.

A form of complete circumference, well rounded from the end of her back to the beginning of her thigh,

It showed from the front as I thought I was Jonny Gill singing My My My.

Every muscle formed perfectly in every part of this beautiful female's leg,

Instantly I went against my manhood, got down on my hands and knees and began to beg.

Since her ankle and toes have never been covered, it matched her semi-red half brown skin,

Standing in perfect form, I looked up; thinking will this silence ever come to an end?

I then asked who she was, but no reply was given, and I asked where she is from but still she refused,

Matching her stature, we stood neck to neck as I looked and felt so confused.

Nothing came from her well-rounded lips but a smile, as I still wasn't convinced,

Being that she is her and I am me, thinking to myself why do I feel so condensed?

So, I closed my eyes, without feeling fear, hoping to come to some kind of conclusion,

She suddenly spoke as she drifted away, saying that she was just my imaginary illusion.

My Matured Love

How could she have done it
raised 8 children and others on her own
her husband passed away so she had no one but her
the cold weather often took her strength
as the summer heat isolated her will to do
day after day she continued to pray
On two black worn out knees
to the Lord above seeking for help
she is described as beautiful as the morning sun
that skin color that mixes cocoa and milk chocolate
and her eyes sparkled vibrantly like the evening star
now that age has invaded the loneliness of her appearance
time spent imagining her younger days I wish I was there
though her voice once provoked is triumphal like an ocean's wave
but still, she manifests her humbleness like a rose during its blossom
Her motivation to do, is allowed by others by her adamant smile
you wouldn't have known if she seen the depth of racism or torn capitalism
The correct persuasion of religion that this world possesses

from believing in something other than what's true

to believe in others when they actually believe in you

I forcefully believe that this person's traits, are everything I desire from a woman.

Love you Grandma Jones

The Protocol Son (To my Dad the day I came home from Jail)

He wasn't the type to show his pain
but I saw it through his smile
his touches became distant
for a second I forgot who he was
when his words injected pain and hurt
I try my best to make him laugh
for no tears ran from his eyes
but happiness was self-destructing inside
He remembered me as clearly as the day
for his smile was something we both were missing
embracing in his arms was his prodigal son
while inside our hearts were kissing.

I Write Only What I See

Her beauty Cleopatra
her abundance of riches
like the Queen of Sheba.
I'm lost in her words
as a ship in the Bermuda Triangle.
I want to escape in her arms
like fugitive to the Mexican border,
but holding me back is her eyes.
She's an improved Medusa,
her strides fall in sequence
as soldiers in a line for war,
I'm smitten by her daily touch, even cotton is surrounded by thorns
Her intelligence influence websters
producing our words of speech,
and if her blood was drawn
for pleasurable taste
the dripping down my face will be the juices
from the sweetest Georgia Peach.
Her touches scan me
but sickness they do not find

rejoicing are my skin cells
Pleased is my soul and mind.
Roses are the curves of her lips
but the pedals never fall off,
for I watered them with appreciation,
and they thanked me in return.
When her presence is wished upon
like the Christmas tree top ornament,
she softly falls on me like Egyptian silk
making me worthless like an antenna when it's bent.
She provides like Blue Cross and Blue Shield
for healing is just the start,
and in my life needed is fresh air,
and like State Farm she's always there.
Sarah Lee must have known
That nobody does it better,
for in my life like under my arms I'm sure.
With her in my life there's no need for the sun,
for our wish not to the sky at night for a star she has become.
Being that the farming industry of Idaho
produce only one thing I also produce one thing,
and that's my unconditional love for her.
Sometimes I feel crippled like the dumb and feeble

and like the FDIC of a business, my duties as a man she can rely on.

Every King should have a Queen

to share his wealth and throne,

and being that my castle is finite it still is my home,

and I want her to always feel welcome and needed,

for I don't want her love to be like

cellular phones and roam.

At times I become afraid because

like legal tender I get used abused and often misused,

I just want my love to be imprinted

on her heart like the way Nike

symbolizes their shoes.

Without her around I feel uncivilized

like a third world country,

she's important to me and I need her

like the states needs their president.

Our communication is crucial like jurors to a trial

and like Massingale to a female

I need her more than once in a while.

From the back of my throat

to the very tip of my tongue,

I want her kisses to reside in me daily

giving me that selfish feeling like Lays
because I just cannot have one.
I want to sip her double shot of espresso
in a hot cherry latte,
I want my kisses to be the sweetness of her sour taste.
I often wish her single touch would
lather me up like Dial or Caress.
Giving me that good feeling like
the flow of hot cocoa through cold blood.
I want her beauty and my sense of humor
to merge like ExxonMobil,
I want our future to be christened
forever humble and blessed.
I would like the heavens and the earth to
meditate on her beauty,
gasping for a drop of her love, misty covered
like the front lawns from the morning dew.
I want the trees to sway in abreast
like the Georgia Mass Choir in concert
when she blesses the earth with her steps.
I want the sequences of the bird's chirp
to make music with her every word
and in the morning her freshly picked rosemary scent,

circulate softly like an aroma

but like Folgers in a cup, she is the best part of my waking up.

My Plea for Help

Lord I know I've done you wrong in the past,

And my future without you, I know will not last.

But I ask you for help, for my mind body and soul,

Giving up these rights, so that you can have total control.

My life is without your guidance and your happiness,

Will bring each day regret for getting myself into this mess.

The question I ask myself, followed by the actions I take,

Undecided about which way to turn or what move shall I make.

So, Lord, I ask you this time to guide and bless the best and worst parts of me,

Open my closed eyes and give me perfect vision to see.

I know that trying to be perfect is strenuous, but I'm doing the best that I can,

Trying not to use loneliness as an excuse or the fact that I am a man.

I have hopes, dreams and in love with a beautiful person,

But following in the tracks of destruction will lead me without the love of you and everyone.

So, now I ask for your hand so that your love and mercy will lead the way,

Guide me through my darkest hour; help me so that I won't go astray.

The Necessity of Love

Alone without someone to kiss,
Alone without someone to miss.
Alone without a simple smile,
Alone without feeling so agile.
Alone without your family or friends,
Alone without knowing if this is the end.
Alone without the thought to care,
Alone without you actually being there.
Alone without love, but enduring the pain,
Alone without comfort but still love remains.
Alone without you because of me,
Alone without freedom, now I am no longer free.
Alone without work but still I am able to survive,
Alone without life but still I feel alive.
Alone without the materialistic things we possess,
Alone without choices now my heart has finally confessed.
Alone without trouble now I see the traps and snares,
Alone without guides therefore I become more prepared.
Alone without incarceration, so I search for no bond,
Alone without right, for in me I can do no wrong.

Alone without the who's, the what's, the dos and the don'ts,

Alone without the why's, the if's, the will's and the won'ts.

Alone without these things is something we often abuse,

Alone without the necessity of love is something we never should take for granted or misuse.

The Dream That Didn't Come True

I wish I could fly as free as the birds,
far and high where I cannot be seen nor heard.
When the air is cool and the temperature is fair,
I'll spread my wings and glide softly through the air.
Now that I am up here I am as free as I can be,
but there still one problem, I'm not really happy.
So, as I fly around constantly looking below,
I see the face of my love, so there I must go!

Amen

Look up O weary eyes
towards a calm sky that is so heavenly,.
Forget about the worries that have bestowed your heart
let them go and remember to let me.
I know there is a battle you now face
but remember joy will come in the end,
please don't give up on your faith
trusting in me as a well-deserved friend.
Call out to me!
For I will answer your every prayer,
situations happen because I have allowed
and know I would not put more on you than you can bear.
You know that my words are true
and with me you can always stand,
but if you put your trust in them instead of me
I will surely release your hand.
So as you go into this unfamiliar land
that I have prepared for thee,
if your vision is blurred and your heart is filled with grief
then the savior you look for you will never see.

The Cheating Writer

My girlfriend caught me cheating
late one Saturday night,
before my mystery date even started
I felt something was not right.
We both had to work
so I knew I could create a plan,
she never doubted my love for her
because she will never stop loving her man.
I have known this person,
before my girlfriend and I became a pair,
in days when my girl didn't have time,
my other chick was always there.
We will have long walks and talks
basically having fun together,
but this secret woman was not like my girl
she will be down for whatever.
I have been with my girl for a while
but I've known my other chick much longer,
while inside I do feel something is wrong
but my love for this other chick is much stronger.

I can never let them cross each other's path
for I know that my girl will fight,
she loves her strong black man with all her heart
but besides her belief, the other chick is white.
I know that interracial relationships are accepted
and people are involved in them from different kinds,
but when those walnut color eyes saw this Hershey colored brother
We both knew that this was the perfect time.
So on this night my girl went out
and my chick came out to play,
excited but scared I continued as planned
for with me she could have her way.
We started in the kitchen, then to the couch
as the excitement led us to the bed,
I never thought I would cheat on my girl
but she wasn't the only thought that ran through my head.
As our playful notions grew louder and louder
we ignore the love making between the keys and the front door,
My patience became short as
This other chick had a different world that I just had to explore.
As the noise from my girlfriend's disbelief, brought our fun to an end
And my girlfriend stood lifeless in her shoes,

she didn't know my love belongs to others

So the question lies, what is a woman to do?

I love to write on white paper!

Is this the End?

If this is the end, then let me say this,
That everything about you, I will truly miss.
Your laugh, your smiles and the happiness within,
Your touch, your love and where your beauty begins.
At times we do things, not knowing in the end if we will feel regret,
Hoping that things will change, causing us altogether to forget.
Yes we laughed, and had the best time ever,
But can we truly say that this is the end, for now, forever?
When I cried for you and the tears burned my outer skin,
It seeped through my pores and now I feel it burning within.
I can't change the hands of time, but I do know this,
That you were my first love, and you will be truly missed.

Food for the Soul

A lighter shade of apple butter,

Soft like tomatoes but will spoil if not covered.

Rich like fully baked homemade bread,

Sweet tasting like corn when mixed with cornbread.

Gently held in my hand like eggs so they won't crack,

Motionless you laid like sliced bread on the oven's rack.

Your apple skin colored hair hung like limbs on a willow tree,

Neatly rounded like a Sunkist orange, oh how I like to taste and see.

Like the juices from a peach uncontrollable and exploding when provoked by my lips,

Honey dew drop, drips constantly when I meditate in between your hips.

And like the mango, it's sweeter once you reach its core,

Being that your core is coconut milky fresh, my body always yearns for more.

I won't stop there, but continue with my journey within,

Long and strong, I entered like a banana but slipped and slid like its skin.

Like tasting an exotic fruit, I heard your moans and sighs,

I pictured a basket filled with fruit when I looked into your eyes.

As my mind retracts to the morning when sugar covered grapefruit was compared to your touch,

Sweet and sour combined in one, I often miss it so much.

Strawberries favor your smile, how infinite it is but carries a bigger punch,

Being that my thoughts of you stick together like other berries sold by the bunch.

I am full of your nectar, I'm pleased to have tasted,

The enjoyment of your fruits are important and like time I dare not to waste it.

Organically we are similarly bonded by structural masses of complied tissues and composed genetics. A force field of endless and immiserate dialects drawn from great minds and positive dream from the foremothers and forefather who once been where we are trying to go. If writing becomes the divinity of my life, then mentally I will prepare and be aware of my future while learning from my unspoken past.

Made in the USA
Middletown, DE
29 November 2025